THE PORT... SE...

Series Titles

We Are Reckless
Christy Prahl

Always a Body
Molly Fuller

Bowed As If Laden With Snow
Megan Wildhood

Silent Letter
Gail Hanlon

New Wilderness
Jenifer DeBellis

Fulgurite
Catherine Kyle

The Body Is Burden and Delight
Sharon White

Bone Country
Linda Nemec Foster

Not Just the Fire
R.B. Simon

Monarch
Heather Bourbeau

The Walk to Cefalù
Lynne Viti

The Found Object Imagines a Life: New and Selected Poems
Mary Catherine Harper

Praise for
We Are Reckless

"Luminous details vault to life in Christy Prahl's *We Are Reckless*. In these stunning and at times surreal poems, desire has six names, Russian dancers spin inside a throat, and a meeting room for lost women stays open seven days a week. Prahl's book investigates the intersection of violence and love, and the animal impulses beating inside us. In poem after poem, I am struck by the startling imagery and bright metaphorical wizardry captured, for example, by a dog described as a "ribcage with hair." The animals depicted here in all their hunger might easily be exchanged for humans: gorging, brutal, fragile, gone. These poems boldly ask how we define a self, a marriage, and a family via eerie and frightening worlds. *We Are Reckless* is a dazzling debut."

—Hadara Bar-Nadav
author of *The New Nudity*

"Like holding an object up to the light and turning it deliberately, carefully, so that it can be seen from all sides, Christy Prahl's poems reveal to us the myriad facets of a female self-in-the-world as she encounters the mystery and pure strangeness of childhood, marriage, family, and the more-than-human. 'There's a density to what I fail to know,' Prahl writes—and yet there's such density, such richness and depth, to what these poems do know, to what they are willing to behold and plumb and speak about. How well they understand Virginia Woolf's assertion that 'nothing was simply one thing.' I love the wild curiosity of this book, its attention to the off-kilter, the liminal, the often unseen and unacknowledged. I love the way nothing is beneath the notice of these searching, pulsing, vibrantly alive poems."

—Kasey Jueds
author of *Keeper* and *The Thicket*

"Christy Prahl's *We Are Reckless* is an ode to the imperfection of our brief lives, a tribute to how we break apart and come back together, complete with beautiful scars. In these poems, Prahl portrays how we speak love—in fields and abandoned cabins, in muttered recipes and the wordless apology of a door opening. Of the deer, Prahl writes 'They eat our flowers in the summer / and we let them / because the sight of them / is a miracle / beyond the survival of our lilies.' Throughout *We Are Reckless*, Prahl tells us to let go of what's pretty and cling to what's true."

—Jessica Walsh
author of *Book of Gods and Grudges*

"Christy Prahl's sparkling collection *We Are Reckless* captures the extra in the ordinary, deep-diving into the familiar moments of life and making them new, and imbuing them with honesty and heart."

—Elizabeth Crane
author of *This Story Will Change*

"The poems in *We Are Reckless* situate us in wild terrain where love grows, dies, and regenerates again with uncontrollable wonder. Christy Prahl has created a collection where what might have been, what was, and what can become appears in white milk rings, the cigarette smoke that was once allowed on airplanes, and sky that breaks open with rain. This collection teems with life!"

—Julie Babcock
author of *Rules for Rearrangement*

"Yes, there is recklessness here—a reckless precision. Christy Prahl's poems take the ordinary act of description and transform it into an experience of abandon. In her hands, the 'skull of a fawn / tiny and ovoid as a mango' or 'a rutted road / lit with sunflowers' become almost unbearable in their freshness, their strangeness. 'All tooth and blood-dressed miracle,' *We Are Reckless* is a book to renew our shared language and our shared world."

—Toby Altman
author of *Discipline Park* and *Arcadia, Indiana*

"Christy Prahl is an expert observer, ushering us with patience to encounters domestic, recollected, and natural. Her work takes great care with its materials, turning an image or a single word so the light hits it from different angles, showing us 'what looks to be a dead raccoon / turns out to be a plaid shirt /wadded against the berm,' and 'farmers in the center of a flattened map /positioning their combines ahead of the sun.' Though these individual poems are at home wherever they go, the collection's seriously-skilled trick is cumulative: having finished *We Are Reckless*, I realized I had been led by Prahl into a state of deep alertness and calm."

—James Capozzi
author of *Country Album* and *Devious Sentiments*

"I made my way through *We Are Reckless* slowly, luxuriantly, savoring each poem at the start of the day. I reveled in Prahl's ability to tell a complicated, memorable story in the span of a page, as well as her sonorous and memorable language. And I loved that so many hard and bright truths were rooted in the real world: the women in *We Are Reckless* sing with Blondie in the car and remember smoking on airplanes; they take shelter from a tornado in a shopping mall while a boy in an Orange Julius uniform prays; they try to make it through a grocery trip without a cart and drop a jar of olives, inviting humiliation but also a kindness that feels profound. What a splendid, enriching collection."

—Laura Moriarty
author of *The Chaperone* and *The Center of Everything*

"'Women, Children, Weather, Beasts.' With the names of each section in her first collection of poems, Christy Prahl is already speaking my language. These poems reach back and throw a handful of pain into the future, which the future catches and crafts into a sometimes tender, sometimes searing poem. Poems like magnifying glasses and confession booths, where we can't stop staring and can't stop listening. Edgy, aching, and brilliantly honest, this is a potent collection I know I will go back to again and again."

—cin salach
author of *Looking for a Soft Place to Land* and *When I am Yes*

"*We Are Reckless* contains poems exploring 'the vapor of everyday life,' as Christy Prahl writes. Love, death, witches, an Olive Garden, and frogs populate these pages in a way that makes it obvious how everything in the world runs together. Prahl's language is guttural and muscled, honest and realistic. This is a book where 'tomatoes ripen to spongy rot,' bison dung brings birds, and a whole poem is made from a dropped jar of olives in the grocery store. These pieces are deserving of attention because all these things deserve attention, and also because Prahl brings them close, and looks hard."

—Bess Cooley
Editor and Founder, *Peatsmoke Journal*

"Rhythmic, funny, knowing, and wise, this elegant and subtle collection explores the simple elements of a meaningful life with great talent and generosity."

—Jeff Deutsch
author of *In Praise of Good Bookstores*

WE ARE RECKLESS

poems

Christy Prahl

Cornerstone Press
Stevens Point, Wisconsin

Cornerstone Press, Stevens Point, Wisconsin 54481
Copyright © 2023 Christy Prahl
www.uwsp.edu/cornerstone

Printed in the United States of America by
Point Print and Design Studio, Stevens Point, Wisconsin

Library of Congress Control Number: 2023937992
ISBN: 978-1-960329-02-8

Cover art: "Untitled" © Robert Bain. Used by permission of the artist.

Cornerstone Press titles are produced in courses and internships offered by the
Department of English at the University of Wisconsin–Stevens Point.

DIRECTOR & PUBLISHER   EXECUTIVE EDITOR
Dr. Ross K. Tangedal   Jeff Snowbarger

SENIOR EDITORS
Lexie Neeley, Monica Swinick, Kala Buttke

PRESS STAFF
Carolyn Czerwinski, Kirsten Faulkner, Hannah Fenrick, Brett Hill, Julia Kaufman,
Kenzie Kierstyn, Eli Masini, Maggie Payson, Lauren Rudesill, Cat Scheinost,
Anthony Thiel, Chloe Verhelst

for John

Contents

— Women —

— Children —

— Weather —

— Beasts —

— Women —

Bumping Into an Old Love at the Olive Garden

You and your mother had that special kind of thing
that goes beyond filial love.
A sexy kind of love.
/Sort of/
Model pretty,
both of you.
She sang torch songs at a strip-mall jazz club on Saturday nights
and lied to keep you out of school
for visits to the surgical museum or Hopewell burial mounds.
There was no air for me in the room
when it was the three of us.

So when you told me, nearly two decades later,
when we accidentally ran into each other
at the same parking-lot restaurant
in some staggering ambush of time
that she had died,
nearly operatic on painkillers
that unfastened you from one another
the last three years of her life,
it broke me
/Sort of/

but also offered a kind of counterweight
to our history of letters written back and forth
under doors.

And those dusty, tarnished kisses
came back into my custody,
like when my estranged older sister
finally sent me the box of baby teeth
she'd been saving for me
in a dresser drawer
forever.

Retreat

The tiny cottage in the woods is abandoned
until the woman whose husband drinks
takes refuge there
after a bender,
without regret.
The woman loves her husband,
and this is how she continues to love him:
fleeing.

When the rye comes out
she heads to the place with the skeletons of mice
swept into the corners.
The freshly dead smell of brassicas
before the molasses of rot sets in.

The woman will linger here for hours.
She may bring a blanket
or bread, a flashlight, a book.
She may stay the night.

She'll watch as freight trains pass
beyond the tall pines.
Flashing boxcar-painted jewels,
covered in cipher,
"Corn Products" at the rear.

A boy died in this cottage
thirty years ago
after getting lost in a freak snowstorm.
His mother, who remembers little else,
still curses the empty cupboards
of this place.

A gunman hid out here
after killing a couple
for the forty dollars in their wallet.
Now he mops floors at Dixon
and once saw the Virgin Mary
in a watermelon rind,
which changed him.

The woman knows none of this.
If she did she might stay away,
but on this night she falls asleep
as bats stir in the eaves.
She'll walk back gingerly in the morning,
returning to the kind and clear-headed man
she believes herself to love,
who will be fixing a leaky faucet
he's been meaning to get to for months.

Mind the Burners

This is the interval
when my husband,
in a separate room,
cooks dinner.
A potato, a leek
baked into a crust
worthy of winter knives
and forks.
He recites the recipe
to himself
and listens to music softly
as the notes
permeate the plaster.
This is the carbon dating of love
after a fight with slammed doors.
No penitence
or stitching back together.
Simply a softening into quiet
once the storm has passed
and spared the roof.
Voices that braid
into an ear.
A potato, a leek
becoming a pie.

Throwaway

How many crows till it counts as a murder?
I tally them with each rotation of my pedals
riding along these misted roads as the sun pinks up.

Fields of chicory and milkweed to one side,
barns held by sodden boards
and a hope for light winds on the other.

A fox crosses the road in front of me.
Small mirages make their way.

Ahead, what looks to be a dead raccoon
turns out to be a plaid shirt
wadded against the berm,
sponged with rain and road grit.

What a puzzle, I think,
how a plaid shirt lands on the side of a country road.

Discarded by a man too much in his heat,
counting to ten like his counselor showed him?

Then it dawns.
Why does the primacy of human thinking
always call to mind a man?

A woman, yes, coming to this singular conclusion:
Fuck it.

Temperatures tilt toward 90 as she tears
at the buttons and frees her skin.

Bare breasts apricot in the full drape of the sun.
Head turns upward toward a rabbit in the stratus
as she dares any cop or church van
or stabled lover
to stop her.

Nelly

I remember being afraid of ghosts.
It was yesterday.
The day before I was sure
we'd run out of milk before the morning's breakfast.
What will become of our stomachs
if we have to drink the coffee black?

I come from the twitch of my father's side,
the house burning down
as he lay teething in a crib,
rescued by the calloused hands of firefighters.

And the rattle of my mother's—
her father vibrating with gin after
returning from the potato fields.

It goes through the blood and into the milk,
woven into bags of apples past their prime.
Today it may be a lump in the arm.
Tomorrow, the invisible
hazards of grass.

Ethnography of a Woman Broken Into Parts

Exhibit A: An oversized wool hat enters the grocery store
with a woman underneath it.

Observe her buying a melon.
Observe her surveying the sharpness of block cheddar cheese.

The woman smiles pertly at toddlers, pretending
to be charmed by their legs swinging from the baskets of grocery cart

dirty fingers fishing
through cereal boxes.

The woman has brought no list.
It's just her after all, and her arms are capacious.

Seized by a sudden desire beyond her vocabulary
the woman chooses prosciutto,

chooses dried apricots,
chooses a jar of pitted Greek olives, which

she balances in her arms
as she chooses dried porcini

then drops the jar of olives on the floor,
cracking open louder than a firearm,

spreading its dark Rorschach across the concrete.
Is it a jellyfish?

No, a plane in free fall.
A butterfly pinned at the wings.

Exhibit B: Two teenage boys with mops arrive
to clean the broken glass and spilled fluid

and any evidence of her.
Observe the way these boys need haircuts.

Observe the woman apologize for the brutality of her presence here,
her crime against grace,

and offer to pay for the olives,
which they accept with indifference.

Observe the way this, and not the breaking of the glass,
or the cleaning of the liquid,

or even the boys themselves and their fragile pubescent striving,
is what makes the woman start to cry.

All that she is—knit woolen hat,
armload of impulse, guarded apology—

she would broker for five minutes back of her life
to choose a grocery cart

and care not at all about the tiny sticky boy who'd sat inside it
before she touched the handle.

Or maybe, observe:
a stranger who hears the commotion

rushing over to help,
smiling gently before saying out loud,

One of those days?
then offering one of the olives from the broken jar.

Look. It's still good.

Call for Volunteers

Today I saw eleven pounds in your face,
heard the heavy elevators in your voice.

You, who iron the sheets
and tend this terrarium filled with miniature turtles,

while your beleaguered husband and children
forget their ham sandwiches for lunch.

You answer phones in the night
and drive your car to retrieve women

on the side of a road
where they rarely show up.

Those that do carry their shoes in their hands.
Some may drag a daughter behind them

proclaiming, *My tooth is loose,*
hoping it will puncture the atmosphere

between that old known life
and this new terror.

You drive home trying to forget their faces,
singing loudly to Blondie as you floor the pedal.

The skunk cabbage on the roadside looks pretty
but smells like rotting food.

You are the opposite. Your face is weary,
but you smell of pine.

What Goes Unseen

How is it that I've come to sleep in the car? An hour ago
we were fine. Even mundane. Playing our favorite board game,
which you were losing, uncharacteristically, and you told me
you no longer cared about this game, at all, so I packed up my tiles
because winning seemed less important than the feeling
of simply being together in this broken universe, perhaps
on the brink of civil war, perhaps on the precipice of fighting for flour,
of finding places outdoors to defecate because plumbing
required more water than we'd been rationed for the week.

Suddenly the packing up of those tiles became the autobiography
of our marriage, and it was terrifying and vast in its emptiness,
so we took out that pain on one another because what other target
did we have? Our last move in the game was *wear* for just 14 points.
Had we continued, I would have added a y.

When You Kiss Me

When you kiss me you get all of me:
the face, the mouth, the fingers.
You get the years of being broken by love.
The irreconcilable ache of this body, alone,
the unshackled heave of its engineering,
the low notes of want.
You get the breath still sour from last night's dinner,
the vitamin deficiency,
the easy bruising,
this map of obsidian veins
embroidered down the backs of my calves.
My grandmother's veins,
passed down.
You get the license to touch me there,
and there,
and there.
Not there.
Not yet.
Just.
Wait.
The fear of guns
and turbulence
and the green clouds that gather chemically
on the horizon
before becoming a tornado,
and church,
and holes,
and frogs.
You get my lips and tongue and throat.
Drive-trains of anger,
cylinders of yes,
giving and receiving

along with you,
working urgently
toward linguistics.
I have something important to tell you.
My desire had six names
before you.

Syntax in the Age of STEM Education

We once studied sentences, poetry, plays,
I tell my nephew, who looks at me with indifference.

We are living in the future,
which, counter to prediction,
holds no flying cars or drones delivering the mail
but is instead very much like the past,
except that our food is manufactured
in a city that was once Cincinnati
and our farm equipment reclassified
as military gear.

Sounds like a waste of time, he says.

Oh, it was, I reply,
remembering the lost ecstasy of wasted time.

I leave him to the device
perpetually flickering light
and woven to the sinews of his hand
knowing that I,
an aging woman with few pleasures left
in these barren afternoons,
can still close the door to my bedroom,
unearth the tattered copy of *My Ántonia*
hidden between the mattress and box spring,
and bring myself to climax
over the detail of a rutted road
lit with sunflowers.

The Editing Window Has Passed

Each night I wake from the swallow of dark dreams:
a meteor slams into the front yard, breaking
our soft bodies into fragments,
folded into the blank space of once existing
but impossible to eulogize.

I'm distracted by the tut-tut of a broken clock
as I fidget next to the sleeping man I hate
or have hated for the last eleven hours,
which is the last we uttered a word to one another.
(A word about who left the milk out to spoil).

He trombones through his nose, immovable
as cement beneath the covers,
while I struggle for a regular cadence of breath
and wonder if it's truly possible
to suffocate a grown man with a pillow.

I'll spend the next hour
rehearsing how to break the silence
without yielding my dignity,
remembering it was I, distracted,
who orphaned the milk to the counter
while scrubbing the refrigerator of ghost rings.

I listen to the metronome
of the clock ticking backwards,
regretting it will never quite
reach yesterday afternoon.

Positioned

She of the tawny ponytail, the lacquered peach toenails peeking through sandals, tenderly. She of the hydrangea bushes, of the godsend Natalia who comes twice a month to tidy the house, of the silver hatchback plugged into the electric socket in the garage—don't put your fingers in there, it will burn your hair to barn straw —of the handmade masks she routinely forgets to carry into the supermarket. She of the Mandarin immersion classes for tiny Amelia, who plays the violin, poorly, to great acclaim. Of the shelter spaniel mix nearly left for dead at Animal Control. Of the inherited Waterford goblet collection (not her style but you can't exactly throw them away), the cities burning on CNN while she bakes a blueberry pie. She of the morning meditation to her dead father's Joni Mitchell LPs, of the industrious red wigglers in the composting bins, the single clean finger checking for polyps inside her panties, snuck sideways for the pleasure she suspects she doesn't deserve.

Milky

A clear morning
before the sun
is air without weather.
Without oversight.
Just . . . supernovas. Planets.
They fall sometimes,
pulled askew by satellites,
surveying what feels like
the last person left in the world.

In the cities there may be a thrum,
but here,
away,
it is lonely in the stillborn
blanket of the thing.

Overhead, a moon, glaring.
A bright light that may be Jupiter.
Stars strung together like diamonds in the teeth.
Children can see them,
drawing lines between that make dead astronomers
articulate again.
Yes, that's the one.
Exactly.

But my shapes are all wrong.
No cup.
No archer.
  The zinnia.
  The biplane.
  The catastrophe.

Cipher for the other things I can't seem to get right.
How do you get a cake to rise in a pan?
How do you set this ringer to silent?
How does a body hold a baby?

There's a density to what I fail to know.
It could fit in a ship,
fill the acreage of the gardens
that hold this building
where we've all come,
all of us—
to be in our sadness together.

They've told us to let go
and they'll catch us before our backs hit the linoleum,
eventually packing us off
with our cargoes of loss
to figure out how to exist in the quiet,
reckless mornings
and the gravity.

Hobbies

The couple has taken up ice skating
on the pond past the spot
where the boy was killed on his bicycle
to pretend they're still in love.
Awkward and unskilled at first
they glide seamlessly now
without buckled ankles
across the surface of frozen mud
divining Sonja Henie
in Oslo
rehearsing for the Olympics
on the brink of world war.
The wife longs more for
Surya Bonaly,
all backward flips and dares,
while the husband is tormented
by the image of the ice-dancing pair
who went into a spin
a half centimeter too close,
the blade of the man's skate
cutting the woman's forehead clear open.
The husband keeps some distance from his wife
just in case.
Sometimes they fall
and mutter You okay?
to one another,
then lever themselves up
and brush off their backsides.
Once in a while they offer a hand to each other
and it feels like love
or some close approximation.
Kindness maybe,

which passes for the same
at this late hour.
And the husband and the wife
lay themselves open to these feelings.
In the husband it is hope,
in the wife, warmth,
and they imagine storing these bookmarks away
in their pockets and under their hats
till next season,
forgetting the hundreds of paralyzed fish
and thousands of dormant frogs
awaiting the thaw
underneath them.

Eureka Springs Meeting Room

is open seven days a week to lost women,
women wanting their humors understood,
lonely women with bats in their mouths.
Those who trust charlatans, despite their best judgement.
Hungry for a piece of bread not stamped out by a machine.
Eager to find three partners for spades.
Atheist women with gaps in their bodies
the shape of God.

Some never had sisters.
Some come for a cup of coffee and stay the rest of their lives.
Some have forgotten how to cut up a chicken.
Others arrive with their lips split and bleeding.
Their husbands may come looking but are not allowed in.
Could I borrow an umbrella?
Is this a legal place to park my car?
Almost all hope their hands will get held.
It's been so long
and their fingers are cold.

MasterClass: Women Speaking

Lesson 1 begins with a warning:
Avoid your usual window-dressing.
Respect the word count.
Refrain from slathering your voice in oil
as you enter your reflections in the space provided.

I am the history of moveable type.
Letter press tiles imprint the back of my teeth.
The tongue rolls over, caught in the Q.

Remington manual ping-pinging to the carriage return.
Mr. Ogilvie spitting his estimations on the Peter Pan collar of my shirt.
This is the worst typing paper I've seen in 35 years.

Exorcise your devils.
Siphon off your quiet rage.

There are Russian dancers in my throat.
Out, you khorovod.

Dogs with distemper,
so many caterpillars translating to moths,
slapping the roof of my mouth for egress.
Out, out, you dogs and moths.

Efface the rising action of your insufferable question marks.

There is the breath of conversation
whiplashed to debate
by a marriage past its angels.
Exhaling takes shape in the cold.

There are angels, too.
Broke free of the purgatory of their tireless do-gooding,
planning for larceny.

Kidnapped

They stole me from the murderous expectations
of a Sunday afternoon, offering a ride home
in their rusted sedan, which I accepted
because they were predictable
in their drip coffee and half-finished bowls
of potato soup, complimenting my shoes
and tipping well.

My directions meant nothing as they drove out past campus,
past the strip malls and auto body shops,
past the hand-painted sign for Devil's Icebox,
then beyond the POW flags and eagles carved from stumps of trees,
swerving to avoid a garter snake stretched across the road.

They drove fast and listened to the radio loud
and I felt deathly afraid
and idiotically alive,
hoping I might be kissed by one of them,
this woman or this man I barely knew,
who seemed to find some curiosity in me
as they drove toward the bluffs and stopped the car.

I falsely protested my landing there,
this swallow of lake
with cranes scooping the algae for minnows.

and the two of them laughed,
knowing they had the keys
and what was I going to do? Walk home?

They asked me for an hour and I gave them two
before I finally gave in to it: the rocky bluffs

& the sun painting the creek in gold fleck
& the sandpipers skidding the glaze of water
& even the guns in the distance,
which had no designs on us
but just a goose or fat squirrel for a camp stove.

My heart calmed from its usual barrage of requirements
as I learned to be still, understanding
there is no veracity in clocks
but the impetus to break them.

The Last Three Rows

We once smoked on airplanes.
My nearly grown children don't believe me when I tell them.
That could set the fuselage on fire.
They have no imagination for what once happened on planes.

There, above the origin of weather,
we watched thunderheads form
over tall cities and hardscrabble company towns,
knowing that far below, at the arc of the Earth,
were thousands of gallons of expired milk,
thousands of babies shrill in teething.

Breath by coiled breath we measured the minutes ahead of us
and the world underneath, its lattice of grain,
its tiny hamlets kindled in dust.
Our trays lay flat in supplication for cubed meat over rice
and a wrapped ginger biscuit.

We smoked to mask the smell
of other people's skin after so many dormant hours.

To evade the stories of Iowa basketball tournaments
from men ungainly and hurriedly shaved.

To invite conversation with that rare dolt
who might whisk us into a cramped bathroom
for a quick knock against the edge of the sink.

These were things that never happened
in the vapor of everyday life.

In everyday life the sun rose and set
as we queued for the Vacant dial on the lavatory door.

Flight attendants consigned to coach gossiped together and
broke open tiny cans of 7 UP with a hiss of carbonation
that nearly made them sneeze.

We felt one with them now,
though we were singular in nothing.

Scores of identical flickers of light on air-traffic screens
hurtling toward Seattle, Cincinnati, Dubai.

We nearly made ourselves dizzy
on swallows of nicotine
and felt large together in a small place.

We clutched our white packs wrapped in cellophane
firmly in our right hands, reassured of their power
as we drifted off,
faces wedged against the cold plastic wall,

worried, momentarily, about geese in the engine
or worse,
that we might be falling out of love with our children,
imagining what else we might have become.

Red House

I imagine myself inside you,
strange little house,

abandoned as a deer blind
in the pitch-husk of night,

your wainscot eroded
nearly to rust, pathologies

exposed to the weather
where the linoleum has cracked

and the dirt breathes up.

That a strong wind hasn't blown you over
is testament to the stubborn will of disrepair.

This disrepair,
which I come to visit on foot

when the day has rubbed me raw.
Yesterday I pulled a two-inch filament

of hair from my cheek
and ruminated for hours

where I'd laid those lost keys.
We must always remember:

We are, all of us,
hurtling toward decline.

Our mouths smell of it, the noises
in our abdomens announce it as we sleep.

This house is just large enough for one,
and I will make a most competent widow.

On the Tip

Don't mind me, declared my mind.
It's cheeky that way,
waking me in the brittle hours of morning
when only the coyotes seem alert to the
Earth's rotation,
the moon like a paper window shade
letting in too much light.

This (once) loved memory, cluttered
with donated furniture,
recliner heaped on loveseat heaped on green velvet couch,
corner shelves crammed with imitation Hummels,
their twee fingers broken off
or dipping into pies.

I wake and can't remember the word for eyelid.
I plead with my husband,
What is this thing I can't force to close?
jarring him awake in a nightly emergency.

Someday, all that forgotten language
will stack up in boxes in the corner of the bedroom.
We will ease open the lids, setting free   an exodus of words
like thousands of tiny barn swallows,
flapping for their lives toward the chimney flue.

Schenectady
telegraph   bulgur wheat
Chariots of Fire   mirepoix   Cartagena
pole barn   antagonist
marsupial   echinacea
tollbooth   Mr. Rochester
filament   pontoon

Feathers cascading down like a curtain,
closing shut over top of me, closing me shut.

One morning my husband will lean over to kiss me
and I'll be helpless to place his face.
I can only hope I'll feel tenderly toward
the stranger wearing his clothes.

Cleaving

When it happens
we will divide this household in half,
all its worldly belongings split in two
toward contractual fairness.
You will keep the cushions of this couch
while I carry its base and casters
which will be better for my napping,
as I enjoy things firm.
You will have the pots,
I, the pans.
A future for you of soup,
for me, eggs.
The towels will be mine and the blankets yours,
so I can clean the filth from this body
and you can dream warm.
We'll argue whether the swear jar
should be divided by value or by type,
I with all the quarters,
you with the rest.
You'll keep the front half of the dog so you
can see her galloping toward you as you
stumble through the back door after dark.
(She thought you'd never get home).
I'll take her hind quarters so she can pill-bug
beside me
on these bones of a sofa.
You will retain the loud shout
needed for televised football games.
I will keep your quiet voice,
the ghost of early love.

Midcentury Sex

Before the world rattles to life, I am here, awake,
indexing us. You could sleep soundly through an act
of war, but I bolt upright to a scuttle of rodents
in the walls, nesting in the fiberglass for warmth.
The things we hear become the things we are.

A train passing through, screaming its urgent whistle
of freight. The clanging emphysema of radiant heat.
We've failed, and we've hurt each other. Sometimes
thoughtlessly, sometimes by design. We've left each
other to a vacant house, alone with the muscle
of our rage. Here, though, in this bone-crushing moment
of a world falling apart, we live in some isosceles miracle
of healing. I reach across and touch your arm,
knowing your body will follow.

— Children —

Jupiter Girl I

The day you stopped running
through the woods after deer
& cut your hair short like
a boy
& dragged the old bicycle
out of your father's shed,
oiled the chain,
pumped oxygen into the tires,
& set off down this
country road
like you were running from something,
your offerings—
string of beads, shark tooth,
Canadian pennies—
left behind to do what offerings do
in the woods,
was the same day
five baby rabbits
we'd been watching since the hatch
showed up dismembered
in the yard.
Severed heads mistaken
by Brown Dog for tennis balls.
Jeweled hearts.
Larvae entrails.
It was a fox that did it.
We'd spied him
three nights strung together
at the perimeter of the woods.
The same woods where we'd watched you
run faster
when you knew
we were looking.

Weekly Constitutional, with Flour and Eggs

There is a souffle in the oven
again.

Our mother tells us not to make a sound
if we know what's good for us.

> *Stop, at once, raising our voices*
> *at each other.*

> *Stop tossing that damn tennis ball*
> *in the hallway.*

November boredom is getting the better of us
in northern lights country.

> *Don't let your feet so much as touch the floor*
> *anywhere past this line.*

(an imaginary arc drawn with her finger
along the parquet)

My sister and I stare at one another,
making cruel faces, comic faces
daring the other to be the first

> *to laugh, to make a peep*

to risk our mother's wagging silent finger (now),
and the slap of her hand (later).
Even the dog goes anemic.

Our mother never liked souffle,
but the peace was a momentary atlas to lost joy.

She cooked them weekly
and fed them to the dog.

Mona's House

Jesus lived on candles in her living room.
Baby with a man's face, swaddled.
Golden halo around the brown hair of a prophet
like the sun clock in the kitchen
that seemed to tick backwards
from the hour we could leave.

We, my sister and I, feared the candles
and the woman who set them on fire
for our visits, who made us pray before
a snack of graham crackers and orange punch.

We, my sister and I, quilted ourselves
small to disappearing,
seeking refuge on our mother's lap,
wishing we could crawl into the pocket
of her shirt, hiding
until she jangled the keys.

Our grandmother had the beard of
a billy goat and a husband
who'd died young of lung disease.

She loved you most when you were far away
and couldn't hurt her twice.

She once surprised us with a song
about a farm woman using clothespins
to turn her skirts into slacks.
We laughed until she said *Be quiet!*
and we realized the song
wasn't supposed to be funny.

Her candles looked down at us
from the mantle, a platform
for Jesus on the cross
and photos of her nephews in uniform,
sporting boys stationed
on the other side of the globe.

They wrote letters
in practiced ink to their aunt,
who preferred boys to
my sister and me, two clinging girls
who didn't understand guns,
or baseball,
or service,
who hated the unvarnished smell of this house.

It smells of old cheese,
we said.
Of morning breath.
Our mother smacked our mouths for insolence
and insisted we come once a month
to visit the woman who raised her alone.

Our grandmother had a French poodle named Pierre
who curled up beside you but bit
when you pet him in the wrong spot.
His entire body
was the wrong spot
most days.

Woodwind

I listen to *Peter and the Wolf*
and imagine myself the duck,
the oboe,
mournful and alive
inside a wolf who forgot to kill me,
sentencing me to an abdomen
full of bottle caps
and squirrel bones.

I ask to play the oboe in the orchestra,
but you tell me the store has just run out,
which is code,
we both know,
for the certainty I will fail at this.
(A child, wet mouth, two reeds)

So instead I become the clarinet,
the common house cat,
an indistinguishable tabby
hiding in dim closets
and under beds.
Contemptuous, drab,
and unseen.

Bodies in Motion, Bodies at Rest

The gymnasium is no place for shenanigans,
sputtered Mr. Click
to the boy and girl under the bleachers.
A random boy with a finger
inside a random girl's pants,
/inside the very girl/
as field hockey drills happened
on one half of a partition
and scoliosis screenings on the other.

And there was I,
cordoned off in the half of the room
that smelled of dough rising,
rubber soles screaming across a lacquered floor,
my collared blouse MacGyvered into a smock
/sleeves tied around the neck,
tails around the waist/
brown plaid fabric with gold flecks covering
my cat-nose breasts,
hunched over like a diver.

Classmates ahead of me
ushered through
swiftly as bottles being stamped.
My bare spine exposed
for its full archaeology
as nurses mused
on the defects
of my body.

I could hide underneath the bleachers,
guiding a boy's finger up, up,

just a little bit higher,
taking the place of the girl
who could bear it only
by imagining Monica Rasmusson,
varsity field hockey forward,
exploring the core of her girlhood
instead.

/Monica Rasmusson with the strong, slender fingers.
Monica Rasmusson who cracked the stick against the ball
with the sound of the world being born/

Or I could trade places with the goalie,
guarding the net in shin guards
and mouth guard,
knowing the ball would land squarely in my abdomen,
vacuuming the breath out of me.

What was scoliosis to a teenage mob
but leprosy?
Another beautiful word for an ugly thing
that made me ugly in its suitcase.

Next Door

The day my dog died
you wore your hair in a bun to a party
and my breath caught at the ways we'd come undone,
once accomplices,
twisting the heads off our dolls
to make monsters.

You, dark hair varnished over your scalp,
sun glinting off a perfect egg,
tiny purse at the end of your fingernails.
Me, the carcass of a cattle dog beside me
after he'd eaten antifreeze that spilled on the floor
of the garage.
Bad dog.

Are you my friend? I'd asked
as we played four-square on the driveway
one boring summer day.
Duh, you'd said
and I hoarded the word like money.

There goes my friend to a party, I thought.
Silver barrette, silver sedan.
Tomorrow I'll ask her to help me bury the dog,
and she'll say that's something a hillbilly would do,
so I'll throw his body in a plastic garbage bag.
The men come to pick up on Thursdays.

Hibiscus

A folio of other,
owned,
used up gas nozzle
of girl/woman.
Underpass bedroom
for the drought version of you,
in you,
childhood brokered
for blankets.
Body etched with age
and purpose.
Your age.
Others' purpose.
Teeth break skin.
Doors latched open
by the hands
that came before.
Loaned parachute,
borrowed dress,
cooked fish.
Your body goes back to you now.
Your spleen. Your clavicle.
Your ankle and hair.
Tomorrow
you will paint your fingernails gold.
You will rub your calves with oil.

No Hands

August is too hot to be alive
and everyone I love is angry with me.
The old bike in the shed
still works.
Pedals rotate,
chain stuck in third gear.
I break it free
expose the rust to air
and leave this terrible farmhouse
with its spiders
and insulation of old rags.
Steam rises from the ribbon of roads.
It will storm tomorrow.
A barn will be hit
by lightning
and collapse.
A small boy
will perish
as he runs from the swing set
to the root cellar,
mesmerized too long
by the clouds and their unfolding.
I turn down roads with names like
Apple
Alice
and Snow.
Family names
from times of blanketing in
and turning the soil.
The sun is down
and this is a place without streetlights
but my tires hug the pavement

as I pick up speed.
I may fall   .
but deserve the slick of ground
on my skin.
The sting of dust and air on a wound.
I take my hands from the bars
and list.
Gravity arcs my body to the road.
My line turns echocardiogram
as the steam of summer heat on asphalt
rises like ghosts.
The grandfather I loved
and the one that I didn't.
For this minute, though, I am squarely alone.
For this minute I don't need anyone at all.

Birthright

The mechanics of this body
have never made a baby.

They once held the start of a baby,
a clot expelled one morning that painted
a rare orchid in my underwear.

> *(The ovaries of the orchid hide behind the flowers.*
> *They may bloom sixteen weeks awaiting pollinators.*
> *Sixteen weeks is a long time to be beautiful).*

I feel your uninvited worry under the skin.
I will shrivel like winter morning glories with no one
to toast a memory of me.

But I long for no soft porridge
in the crook of my elbows.
A baby's head smells to me not of nostalgia
but of Wednesday's curdled milk.

> *(Elliot Meckler saw a spot of blood on my skirt*
> *and called me Bloody Mary the next seven years)*

Please, everyone else, pass this newborn around
as I've just discovered a perfectly good dog that needs lifting.

A dachshund will reliably fall asleep in my arms,
but even a barely sentient baby can decode a woman's
fear of not supporting the neck.

Modern Witch

I carry my sin swimming
through the muck of a river
choked with algae,
glazed with moss,
thick with dying salamanders.
You, elder statesmen of cul de sacs,
will try to sink me in creekwater.
You will stamp like marionettes when you fail.

You believe I stole your firstborn
from calculus class,
but let me assure you
it was she who found me.
Through the serviceberry,
through the nettles
to the Airstream in the woods
where I broil fish for dinner,
just like you.

She visits each afternoon,
scorned by lab partners,
underestimated by teachers
who call her apoplectic.

She has mastered the alchemy of pine tinctures
and now melts ryegrass and golf balls
over a fire in the yard.
She's learning incantations,
so it's best you be dressed.

These Things Impossible

I was the girl you loved
before you stopped loving girls.
An experiment that fooled me
for maybe a month.
You were the boy
who wrote a song for me on the piano
and played it on stage
to the cheers of your classmates
who loved you,
who still,
from time to time,
leave copies of playbills at your family plot
where your full name,
which no one called you,
is inscribed like the quilt that hangs
in the Smithsonian
behind glass
inert as you were
those last days,
body ravaged by disease,
face smeared with plums.
I had understood later, of course,
why you left me,
and knew there was a part of you
beyond sex,
beyond gender,
that still remembered kissing me
with fondness.
And I went home
and wrote your name in the garlic skins
that had gathered in the metal bins
in my mother's pantry.
I tossed them into the wind,
believing that might keep you alive
on the lungs of the planet.

Hello

Pam the babysitter
hit us with wooden spoons
for leaving our dolls
scattered across the basement floor,
or gripping two small hands
around a glass of milk.
Mind your manners,
she admonished my knuckles.

One strange afternoon
a skywriter overhead,
and all of us in the building,

> the old couple on the ground floor
> who stole the morning newspapers,

> tall Joe across the hall who sang along to Puccini records,

> the twins with the long blond hair
> who weren't allowed to play with us on Sundays,

> my parents, my sister, and I,

> and Pam, down the way,
> waving like any close friend might do,

craned our necks upward
to watch this small miracle of a Saturday afternoon.
Out of airplane exhaust
looped the word *hi.*
He'd seen us.

Levee

Count the cars of the freight train that idles you,
bushels of corn followed by stacks of lumber,
graffiti animated by zoetrope as this baby,
your first,
crowns between your legs.
Full muscle curls your birthing daughter to a fist,
urging her back from the noisy world long enough
to be caught alive by a midwife.
72, 73, 74, . . . 89,
harvesting the power
of your ponderous body
and her small hand
for all they will be forced to carry.

— Weather —

Reclaimed by the Ice

When it snows I think of Nathan,
walking with assurance
over gravel, over frost,
consuming whole the polar expanse of Iceland,
its green leas to its white-dusted mountains,
cracked clean, surrounded by sea.

His footing holds as a squall picks up.
A map suddenly erased of its landmarks.
North and south in matching jackets.

He is out of provisions
for this walk that was to occupy an afternoon.
Layered in down, but only for daylight
and not the frozen box this place becomes by nightfall.

I think of him casually
shaking his compass for answers,
imagining the coffee at the ranger station
and the story told through numbed lips, breathless
with dumb luck.
I think of the sun falling on the horizon
as he surrenders to spending the night here,
laboring to build an ice cave
with the last of the air in his lungs,
calculating whether to continue
or use his reservoir to stamp an SOS in the snow.

Fighting at first,
then settling into the clarity
of what is forcefully,
quietly,
happening to him.

I think of him retracing his footsteps to add a new message:
AT PEACE,
which the snow will fill within the hour.

His professors planted a tree for him at Harvard.
It's lost among the other trees,
as Nathan would have preferred it,
but tall enough to stand beneath
for shelter.

Middle Night

No joy in knowing 3:20 in the morning.
Ask the bus driver saddled with third shift;
she'll tell you.
The derelict loneliness,
the empty seats,
the ones and twos
who mumble to themselves indecipherably,
possibly, she fears, how to take their own lives,
or hers.

Ask a woman in labor,
groping in the darkness for her shoes.

Ask the insomniac
swallowed inside a cloakroom,
so many buttons to count.

Ask a pilot over Nebraska.
No jigsawed fields of soybean,
no pinwheeling turbines
to break up the navigation
and the nuts have gone stale.

Ask me and I may collapse into you,
begging for a secret.
How do you make the heart slow down?
How do you help your body
remember how to rest?

Don't even think of asking the overnight security guard.
You won't like his answer.

Late Season

Inches from me
you may not know the wanting
of my hand, illegible on your heaving back,
touching you as you sleep, or pretend to.
(Your days are long and pile up).
It's possible the dog is in bed between us,
where you've invited her.
I may reach across
after an uneasy dream,
terrible men on the stairs, approaching,
a missed final exam that has ruined me.
And I'll want you.
Not all of you,
but just a moment of you.
Not your entire body,
not the sex of you,
but possibly your arm
or the crook of your bent leg
reaching across to meet my skin.
To say, I am here, and whole.
I can see you falling, my love.
Watch my hands fold together
as a basket.

April Thaw

When the frost broke
so did my body.
You took tweezers to the tick in my shoulder
and now my hips predict when rain is coming.

My mother has moved far away.
I can't picture her face anymore
from memory.

My dearest and I are fighting again.
The wood was improperly stacked for next winter.

My friendships don't stick.

My lungs have gone asthmatic with worry
for the world,
for myself.

I am quietly selfish.

When we talk of bigotry and the extinction of the bees,
I'm distracted by lost combs and grocery lists,
the ways I've been disappointed by people
and disappointed them back.

The boy at my office
who thinks first of the world
asks,
Where can I put my body so it does no harm?
There is no punchline to this riddle.
Oh,
you sweet idiot,
bodies do harm.

Flesh and bones are thick at this party.
A television screen eternally on,
the only way to chime music into the room
in this age of cluttered information.

I've lost you, dear one, in the crowd.
You can breathe again in the distance,
I suspect.
I hear you laughing but can't find your hat.
And I've run out of words to shout
at these kind people I barely know.

I smile and I drink.
And somewhere from this rat king of arms intertwined
comes your hand.
I can distinguish it from the other hands.
This is a hand that I know.

I'm ready to head home early, you say.
And I read this as the most profound act of love.

Summer Twilight in Buchanan

It is the season of the monarchs
and garden toads,
the berries ripe on the side of the road,
young girls cradling them in their skirts,
failing to pay,
presenting them to their party host
like pearls surprisingly found
in an oyster.
The season of
Virginia creeper caulking its
serpentine limbs
over the dying oak.
The garden party of I want you
later this night lovers
sitting closely in a wicker chair,
tiny green inchworm
weaving a trail through the batting.
The pretty woman wears a braid
her sweetheart holds
like a paintbrush.
Soft tack of arms and legs
honeyed with sweat,
left too long in the sun.
Brand new minted nickel
of love.
The residue of their ardor
broken by the fat man
with the drum in his laugh
arriving uninvited,
making an ugly joke about shrunken heads
in Ecuador.
His Adam's apple
bobbing up and down his neck

as he heaves with phlegm and
claims the chair where the lovers sat
minutes before.
Even he is slicked with desire.
In two hours it will be time to water the garden,
the lilies closing as the sun
drifts down,
only a few stragglers left
to help with the dishes.
They were all just passing through,
tipsy with want,
before the fault line of late summer
spilled the juice from the berries,
stained the skirts,
dropped seeds to the soil
to come up again
next season.

Afternoon at the Beach Before the Storm

Slate
washes ashore
with the patina
of old maps of Michigan.
Gulls scream in formation
at the promise of discarded bread
and fear of oncoming thunder.
It's late July
and mist rises,
vaporizing phantom ships in the distance,
veiled,
primordial,
like they've been keeping watch
on the shoreline since Moses.
They disappear now
into the space
where land, air, and water meet.
Weather swallowing boats
at the end of the world.

Dinner in the Afterward

We'll soon think nothing of these strange times.

We've learned to tolerate their puncture wounds and reckless indiscretions.

We no longer turn away from a dead deer on the side of the road but glance at its entrails and know this wasn't a quiet way to go. Spliced open for the curious to see what helps a doe leap over a leaf pile with such arcing, instinctual grace.

It's right there in the spleen—in the shameless exhibit of blood and bone.

Remember when eating dinner out with friends was a way to spend an evening? We squandered the contents of hours and thought nothing of the cost. We laughed at cruel jokes and touched the forearms of those adrift in their attention.

We'll see our familiars around a table again soon, minus those who migrated west because our worry put a broken broom between us.

We may crawl inside our black dresses and forget how our mouths deliver words.

We'll cry inconsolably over spilled salt and its archive of terrible luck.

We will step giant into this new way of being, knowing at least one among us is now allergic to wheat.

Daily Forecast

I read the weather like some
read the moles
on their lover's backs.
Cumulonimbus will bring a break and a beating.
I'm not afraid.
I see the icons of sun, cloud,
bolt of fire from cloud,
like a necklace strung of tiny charms
raided from my grandmother's jewelry tray.
She loved storms.
She grew prize peonies.
Pruned them back to full flower,
and for one short week they were ciphers
for her breasts.
Full, pink, and wanting,
till they faded to brown death
petals falling in a circle
along the soil, around the brush,
like an offering
that begged for more rain.

When the Sky Turns Green

That spring the tornadoes came twice.

The first while we were at the shopping mall,
my mother, sister, and I, trying on swimsuits
while my father sat on a bench near a fountain full of coins,
and the siren wailed before we could pay.

We took cover in the lower-level food court
as a boy in an Orange Julius uniform
prayed out loud and I wished he would just be quiet
so the funnel could land on someone else's mall.

The second time, early in the morning,
while my sister and I slept in twin beds
in our shared bedroom on the third floor
of the Fairhaven Apartment complex.

We joined the other groggy families in the laundry room.
The mothers, fathers, children,
and all the illegal kittens, hamsters, and bearded dragons
while the landlords looked the other way,
as we'd all looked the other way
the day they paraded their crying six-year-old
through the courtyard in a diaper
because he'd left an accident in the bed.

We made ourselves small at the sound of a freight train overhead
and imagined our sofas, coffee mugs, and Chinese checkerboard sets
sucked into the sky and dropped a mile down the road in one piece.

Later, on the news,
a gunmetal triangle danced against the drunk horizon,
smithereened rooftops, garages, and trailer parks
as the anchorman kept repeating, *Such a shame.*
I realized then that destruction was impetuous,
and fickle, and not without its bigotry.

Wide Open

Hey city girl, you must go to a field.
See the bison if you live to the west.
They low and roam,
sexually unrepentant after flirting with extinction.
Their dung will bring back birds,
which bring back butterflies,
which bring back fertility itself.

If you live in the Midwest,
looking out on
biographies of skyscrapers,
even as fog occasionally swallows them whole,
then, too, go to a field.
In November sandhill cranes land in congregations,
pausing on their way to the Rio Grande Valley,
legs dangled earthward for landing.
Wheels down.
On cold days they huddle,
constricting blood vessels
to make their bodies into coats.
On warm days they spread out
like fractals.

And if you live in the east,
in a chokehold of smog and idling cars,
you, especially, must visit a field,
alive with lavender
and children playing penny whistles
for indifferent cows.

In Hiding

We learned to sit quietly in a room together,
watching a Cooper's hawk out the window,
stoic and unperturbed,
scan the woodpile for mice.

We often wore the same pair of socks
five days running,
daytime sewn seamlessly into bed,
with no concern for the tack
of our bodies.

We could light a fire from last night's ash
and walk steady on ice.
My hair grew long,
your beard unruly.
We tethered ourselves to the intricacies
of yeast, dough rising in the furnace room
as the heat clicked on.

Our restaurants closed
and our friends became our distant friends.
We pruned our families back
to the cambium.

I came to love sardines
from the tin, oily
hairline bones
caught in the teeth.

We could cook a dinner
from pantry scraps.
Caved onions,
flour undulating with worms,
the rind of this cheese.

We had ourselves
and each other
and wanted for nothing.

August Swelter, Bloomington 1986

Late summer, there in the trough of Indiana,
    we girls could barely stand the
        touch of fabric on our bodies

so wore dresses a yard past
    cotton handkerchiefs,
        transparent straight through.

Nostalgia limbo-ed us under the heat
    with our Mary Janes,
        spinning the playground roundabouts

as we walked beyond campus,
    through the park full of crust punks,
        past the Von Lee Theater—

Night of the Creeps on the marquis—
    beyond the sweet shop selling cinnamon buns
        and Korean food, to Ladyman's Café

for air conditioning. We crammed
    seven of us to a booth, skin touching,
        stuck together with the sugar of our sweat.

Utterly golden and alive,
    we felt the eyes of raptors
        on the bronze of our arms.

We were our most terrible and wicked,
    sharing two plates of fries
        and all the free refills on soda to quench us,

then tipping with coins. On the way home
I bumped into you on a children's slide
and you asked if you could kiss me.

You wrapped your pinky around mine
when I said no
and the sky broke open with rain.

Last Night of the Year

Light is a reliable bully through the trees
whether fragments of moon
or traffic
or the overhead bulbs
of restaurant parking lots.

We curse the intrusion
while reading the night-sky Braille together
and booking promises
to carry into tomorrow.

Why raft such fruitless rituals,
we wonder out loud,
drunk on slurry, fat on cheese.
So much foolishness from a foolish species.
Deer and opossum go on about their business
like any other night.

Squint hard to the left and behind to see them,
foraging and fucking as animals do.

We too, animals,
will fail to eat less and bicycle more.
Our accounts, as before, will oxidize to flake.

The dresser drawers will bulge of overstuffed
knit shirts and loose socks caught in back
as we shove and shove and shove
and postpone this latching to another day.

The Pinking Hour

This is my song to the quiet morning. To waking
in the dark when most are still sleeping,
save the revelers heading home from yellow beer
and a clip of conversation
they hoped might lead to sex.

We form a sisterhood, we salted thieves of time.
The early shifters, tucking into uniform. The farmers
in the center of a flattened map,
positioning their combines ahead of the sun.
Hold still its punctuation:
soft paintbrush of a single car driving by,
dog barking for the notice of someone who might feed him,
the movement of planets hung precariously in the sky.

We'll steal another deep breath before turning on the light,
before inviting the din of anchormen,
of backpacks slung to noisy children.
We'll welcome the world's laryngitis
before the treasonous clatter of day.

— Beasts —

The Things That Collect in the Corner That Are Not Mouse Droppings

Sometimes flecks of paint
or food
remind us winter has settled in again,
and with that,
the mice,
the seasonal battle for dominion
and reminder that our opposable thumbs
mean nothing in small spaces.

Sometimes it is merely cobwebs
and the ants they've trapped,
wings of flies,
a carcass of a blue beetle.
All those legs,
weaving their sticky filaments,
trapping atoms of humanity and dust
into this decaying house.

Often, though, it is something else.
That harrowing feeling
that something has gone irretrievably wrong in the world.

It may, at times, be the vestiges of early intimacy,
savage and hungry,
sometimes cruel with want.
The kitchen tables,
commuter trains,
the time I bit the first initial
of my first name
into your back
to make you mine for life.

Or it may be the residue of my mother in the hospital,
not because she'd fractured a bone
but because she'd forgotten to feed the cat for three full
days.

Sometimes, though, it is in fact a mouse
prostrate in a trap
embarrassed by its rigor mortis,
its underside an amusement to history.

Trace It Back to the Animals

It starts in the throat,
sinker and rod
caught on a fish
flailing for   breath
through gills rotting away
to thrush.
Maybe more bird than fish,
more flutter,
caught in a chimney of
creosote,
soot.
Is this the illness or the sleight
of illness?

Isn't there a hotline for this?
The one that sends a runaway home
or tells how to baste
the turkey
to a golden crispness?
The one that pronounces me
not dead.
Still fish.
Still bird.
Animal, not food.
Don't let the dog do her licking.
She'll take it on the tongue.
Her coughs may
boomerang it back.
No one knows.

My body heats like a boiled egg.
Gills, wing, sulfur.

I stand too quickly
and the room goes kaleidoscope.
Ceiling is floor,
floor is temperature.
And what does it matter if we're unwell
if this is the way alive is cooked?

Venison

The dog finds it first.
Tufts of brindled hair in the woods
like wreckage discarded from a brush.

Then the pelts
            picked dry by turkey vultures.

A single hoof comes next
            and we know now to mourn a deer.

They eat our flowers in the summer
and we let them
because the sight of them
is a miracle beyond
            the survival of our lilies.

Finally,
skull of a fawn,
tiny and ovoid as a mango.

Hard study in evolution's
finer points.
Teeth bloody from the fight she gave.
Eyes glistening in decomposition
but somehow
still staring at me.

Carpenters

They arrive with summer heat in tiny destructive armies,
agglomerating on discarded bits of cookie, forgotten kibble,
empty shakers of tequila. Burrowing their tunnels
between floorboards and drywall, scuttling up the drain,
up the flat metal plank of the refrigerator. All head,
abdomen, thorax, mandible, building their colonies in the
seam where wall meets floor meets window where tomatoes
ripen to spongy rot. They carry crusts of bread forty times
their size. They may outwit a depleted woman to collapsing.
They will mount a grain of sugar as if they were kings.

Trying to Explain My Fear of Frogs

We were hunters in the window wells
where the frogs heaved in clusters after a rain.

My sister and I spent our summer here
near the river slicked with paisley green moss,

hummed with August mayflies,
giving our parents the space to split open
and zipper back whole.

I would try on my grandmother's jewelry to pass the time.
Such squinting boredom in those long pink halls
and those long, disobedient hours.

That hour there were no frogs
until there was one frog
carried inside by my sister's cupped hands.

One muscular frog,
and there, my grandmother doing the dishes,
hands chafed to bloody batik.

One frog,
and the specter of a man from Poughkeepsie
who slept late into the morning on our sofa
while our father traveled back and forth on business to
Minnesota.

One frog that hopped from my sister's small fists
and into the foyer, legs
pumping across the footprint of this house.

My grandmother, lover of nearly all things,
yelling without mercy at my sister,
kneading my arm to mulch.

One frog in all the grotesque musculature of its form,
jettisoning across a linoleum floor,
drunk on lemon cleanser.

My grandmother shouting like a sea witch,
jagged fingernails embedded in my arm,
latched like we might never go home.

Dead Animal Season

When the planet forgot its name,
we moved our city lives to the country,
reasoning that if our days were short,
we would live them in the wide open
among the trees and yellow finches.

We cascaded into the rhythm
of our country lives, the mildew gathered in the corner
of our country bathroom, the sound
of copulating mice in the country walls.
And the ticks,
as we combed our scalps with the tips of our fingers
and checked each other's unseen parts.

We heralded fawn season as one of the scientific miracles
of nature, a periscope into the certainty that life persists
even as hundreds of thousands of lungs fail to draw oxygen.

Our favorite farmer used a shotgun
to provide us pork chops for dinner.
He taught us that the color of the chicken
has no bearing on the color of the egg.
It's the chicken's ears that
hold the paint.

Nothing prepared us for the grace
of a deer in motion, crossing the road,
seconds before colliding with an SUV.

Or the trail of sparrow feathers
after an unfair fight with a hawk.
J would say nature has a way of taking care of itself,
so I made room to hate nature:

Its fickle thirst for blood,
its disregard for the way accidental love will
unassailably disappoint us.

On the Eve of Sadie Dying

The gut of this dog
is a shipwreck
of oak leaves,
acorns,
evergreen needles—
her notion of dinner
after rejecting the chicken
boiled for her by hand,
then fruitlessly coaxed to her muzzle.
Bulimic,
she will heave and wretch,
rid herself of
the goblins
of a body
seven times its age.
Shutting down.
Giving in.
She is less mammal
than rib cage with hair.
Discarded brush for a
fright wig.
The organs will go next
but not today.
Today we'll clean her waste
from the rugs,
her scat from the blanket
that doubles as a bed
for this dog that still demands to play.
Who jumps up at the sight of a rubber ball
to signal
I am alive
and pure love.

Porch Raccoons

Less animal than anima,
peeking out of a walnut tree
at 5am
in my city backyard.
Your faces mascara'd,
petrified and staring,
as you scavenge for breakfast
through postage stamp yards
and filthy alleys
sullied by unwanted dresses
and orange peels.

You consort with squirrels in the dark,
eyes gleaming,
thumbs positioned for a fight,
eventually tucking your babies
into the crevice of the tree
so they sleep
without danger of falling
and prepare
for their savage educations.

I didn't expect to see you here
and might nearly be enamored,
but you stole my tomatoes,
you fuckers.

They Can Smell Water

The night splits open
as a single coyote descends a grassy hill,
preferring solitude
to the showy displays
of troops of whitetail deer
devouring birch leaves.

The bitch wants muscle.
I hear her shriek through the elms,
waking me from a dream
I immediately forget,
trading the deep orange and blue of sleep
for this eavesdrop
into hunger and gasp.

All tooth and blood-dressed miracle
of woods,
scrapyards,
train tracks,
creek beds,
backyards with sleeping babies inside.
(Please don't forget to bring in the dog).

By morning slow rabbits will be dismembered
across the yard.
The crows will eat what's left behind.
A child will find a foot and feel lucky.

On Cooking a Chicken

It should bring no joy,
this eating of birds.
Thirty sexless bodies to a cage,
fat with injection, clayed with dung.
Their consumption a filthy thing
with feathers.

Tonight though, nearly bereft
over the loose threads of the world
I braised a whole chicken
  its bones
   & its breasts
   & its neck
   & its gizzards
for an hour,
perfuming the house with game.

Its skin the sag of an aging man,
broth distilled as the hearts of liquor,
flesh broken down between my teeth like all
evolution had ever asked of me

  & now I am sated.
  & now I feel I can shovel the snow
  & now I may watch the news
without disintegrating.

Jupiter Girl II

You know how to pet a deer? she riddled,
pulling up on her bright yellow bicycle.
Go into the woods and act like them
and they'll eat acorns straight from your hand.

Acknowledgments

With gratitude to the following journals for publishing many of the pieces in this collection, some in earlier versions.

"Retreat," *The Bangalore Review*, Volume 8, Issue 7, September 2020

"Mind the Burners," "Breakwater," "Midcentury Sex," *Eastern Iowa Review*, Issue 15, May 2022

"Throwaway," *Passengers Journal*, Volume 3, Issue 1, March 2022

"Ethnography of a Woman Broken into Parts," West *Trestle Review*, November & December 2022

"What Goes Unseen," *Boston Literary Magazine*, October 2020

"When You Kiss Me," *Eunoia Review*, March 5, 2021

"Positioned," *High Shelf Press*, Issue XXVII, February 2021

"Milky," *New Reader Magazine*, Volume 5, Issue 19, September 2022

"Hobbies," *The Blue Mountain Review*, Issue 17, February 15, 2020

"Cleaving," and "The Things That Collect in the Corners That are Not Mouse Droppings," *Cathexis Northwest Press*, September 1, 2019

"On the Tip," and "Birthright," *Broadkill Review*, April 2022

"Hibiscus" and "Late Season": *eMerge*, Issue 7, Summer 2020

"Next Door," *Ghost City Review*, March 2021

"Mona's House," *Writer's Foundry Review*, Issue 1, September 2022

"Reclaimed by the Ice," *Clementine Unbound*, October 5, 2021

"Middle Night," *Eunoia Review*, March 4, 2021

"April Thaw," *Twyckenham Notes*, Issue 11, Spring 2020

"Afternoon at the Beach Before the Storm," *eMerge*, Issue 8, Fall 2020

"Daily Forecast," *The Drabble*, July 31, 2021

"The Pinking Hour," *Unbroken*, Issue 31, October 2021

"Trace It Back to the Animals," *Peatsmoke Journal*, Spring 2021

Without the love, guidance, and support of so many, this collection would not have been born. Fire lanterns of gratitude to my teachers, kindred spirits, and creative partners in crime Tracy Floreani, Anne Hensley, Tom Lorenz, Speer Morgan, Kim Shaw, Amy Stuber, Leslie Von Holten, and Chelsea Voulgares. Unwavering thanks to the hardworking staffs of Ragdale and the Writers Colony at Dairy Hollow, quiet havens that provided me the respite to make writing an active verb. To my mother, father, and sister, thank you for challenging me to be my best and loving me even when I fell short. To everyone who ever read a piece at PenRF, you gave me life and kept me going, and there is no way to fully express my gratitude. To Dr. Ross Tangedal, Brett Hill, Carolyn Czerwinski, and the entire team at Cornerstone Press, thank you beyond words for believing in my work. And to John, my first reader and most cherished and trusted editor, I never felt lost before you, but I'm eternally found when I'm with you.

CHRISTY PRAHL is a Best of the Net and Pushcart Prize nominee whose work has appeared in a host of national and international journals. She has held residencies at both Ragdale and The Writers Colony at Dairy Hollow and is the founder and director of the PenRF reading series. She splits her time between Chicago and rural Michigan.